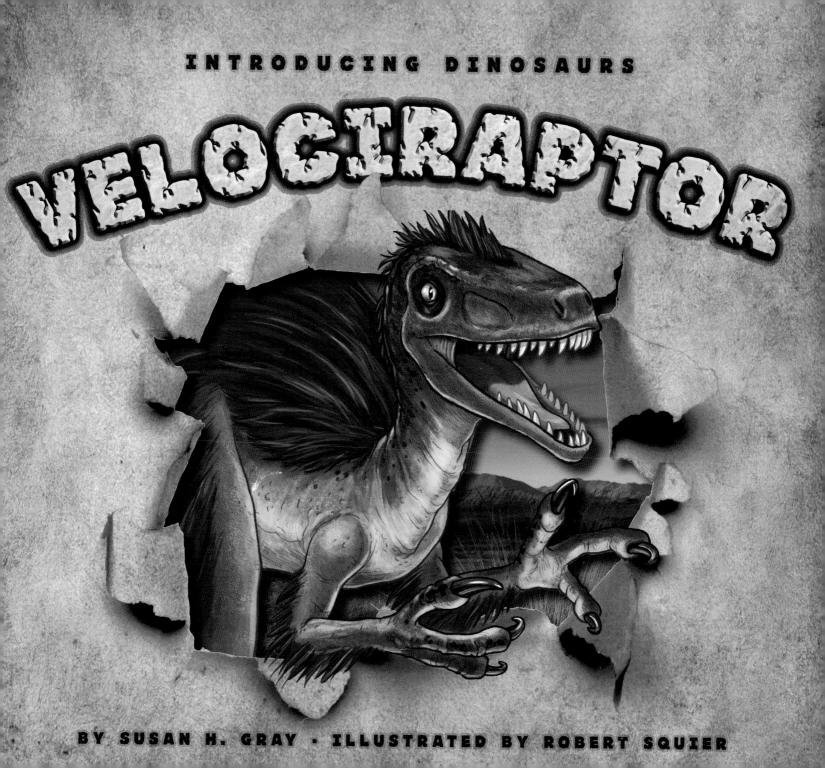

INTRODUCING DINOSAURS

VELOCIRAPTOR

BY SUSAN H. GRAY · ILLUSTRATED BY ROBERT SQUIER

The Child's World

Published by The Child's World®
1980 Lookout Drive • Mankato, MN 56003-1705
800-599-READ • www.childsworld.com

ACKNOWLEDGMENTS

The Child's World®: Mary Berendes, Publishing Director
The Design Lab: Kathleen Petelinsek, Art Direction and Design;
Victoria Stanley and Anna Petelinsek, Page Production
Editorial Directions: E. Russell Primm, Editor; Lucia Raatma, Copy Editor;
Dina Rubin, Proofreader; Tim Griffin, Indexer

PHOTO CREDITS

©Dmitryp/Dreamstime.com: cover, 2–3; ©Francois Gohier/Gaston Design/
Photo Researchers, Inc.: 7; ©Vo Trung Dung/Corbis Sygma: 8; ©AFP Photo/
D. Finnen, American Museum of Natural History/Getty Images: 10–11;
©Tom Bean/Corbis: 12; ©Laski Diffusion/EastNews/Liaison/Getty Images:
16 (left); ©David Muench/Corbis: 16–17; ©Francois Gohier/Corbis: 18–19

LIBRARY OF CONGRESS CATALOGING-IN-PUBLICATION DATA
Gray, Susan Heinrichs.
  Velociraptor / by Susan H. Gray; illustrated by Robert Squier.
     p. cm.— (Introducing dinosaurs)
  Includes bibliographical references and index.
  ISBN 978-1-60253-245-8 (lib. bound: alk. paper)
  1. Velociraptor—Juvenile literature. I. Squier, Robert, ill. II. Title. III. Series.
  QE862.S3G6962 2009
    567.912—dc22   2009001633

Printed in the United States of America
Mankato, Minnesota
December, 2009
PA02038

TABLE OF CONTENTS

WHAT WAS VELOCIRAPTOR?

Velociraptor (vuh-LAHS-ih-rap-tur) was a small dinosaur. Its name means "quick **thief**." *Velociraptor* was certainly quick. It had strong legs, and it was a fast runner. But no one really knows whether it was a thief. Thieves steal things, such as food. *Velociraptor* probably caught its own food.

Velociraptor *didn't have to worry about other dinosaurs chasing it. It could outrun almost anything!*

WHAT DID VELOCIRAPTOR LOOK LIKE?

Velociraptor was not very big. It weighed about the same as a child in the second grade. It had a big head and a mouth loaded with sharp teeth.

Velociraptor's small size is one reason it was so fast. Its sharp teeth tell us that it was a meat eater.

Velociraptor ran around on two legs. It held its tail up off the ground as it ran. This helped the speedy dinosaur to keep its balance.

Velociraptor's hands and feet had sharp claws. Each foot had one especially big claw. **Scientists** sometimes call it the killing claw. It was one powerful weapon!

We know about Velociraptor*'s claws from the bones scientists have found (above). The foot claws were like giant knives!*

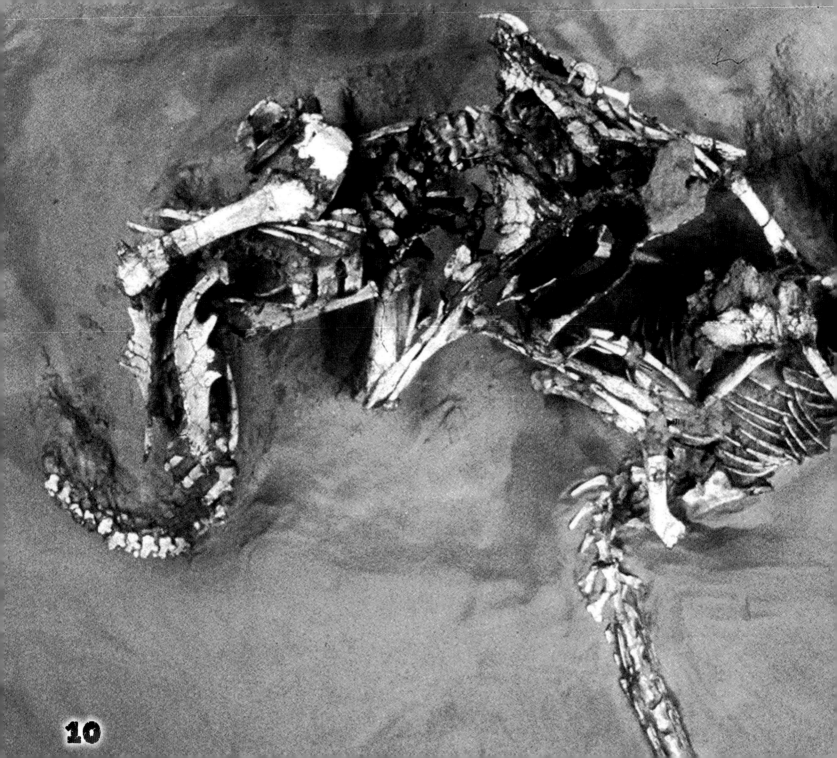

10

WHAT ABOUT THOSE CLAWS?

The killing claw was on the second toe of each foot. It was curved and very sharp. When *Velociraptor* ran, it held that toe up. The claw did not touch the ground. But when *Velociraptor* jumped on its **prey**, look out! Down came that claw! In one swift move, the killing claw did its work.

These bones show Velociraptor *fighting a* Protoceratops *(pro-toe-SAYR-uh-tops).* Protoceratops *was no match for* Velociraptor's *sharp claws!*

HOW DID *VELOCIRAPTOR* SPEND ITS DAY?

Velociraptor spent part of its day hunting. It trotted along, looking this way and that. Maybe a group of *Velociraptors* hunted together.

Scientists study preserved dinosaur footprints to learn how fast some dinosaurs moved. The footprints above are near Cameron, Arizona.

13

When a group of *Velociraptors* saw a slow dinosaur, they swarmed over it. They bit and clawed until the **beast** fell over. Then they stuffed themselves with fresh meat. After that, they might not have eaten again for days!

Velociraptor groups used teamwork to take down much bigger dinosaurs.

HOW DO WE KNOW ABOUT *VELOCIRAPTOR*?

All of the dinosaurs died out millions of years ago. Most of them just rotted away. But some dinosaur **fossils** are still around.

Scientists have found many Velociraptor fossils. Fossilized dinosaur eggs, such as this one (above), are among the rarest of fossils. Bone beds, such as this one in Colorado, tell scientists much about how dinosaurs lived and died.

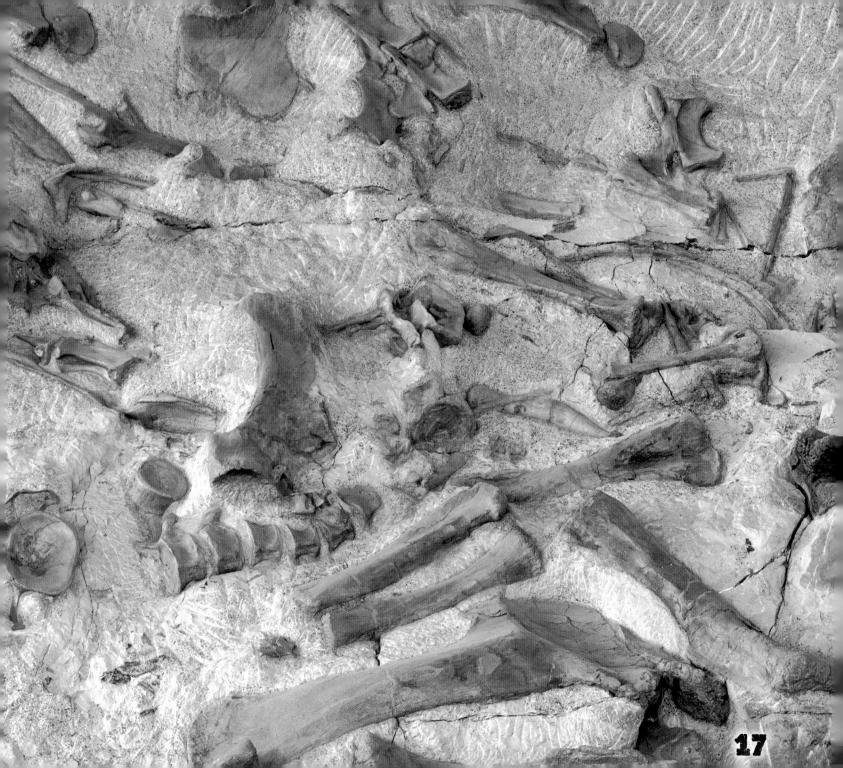

17

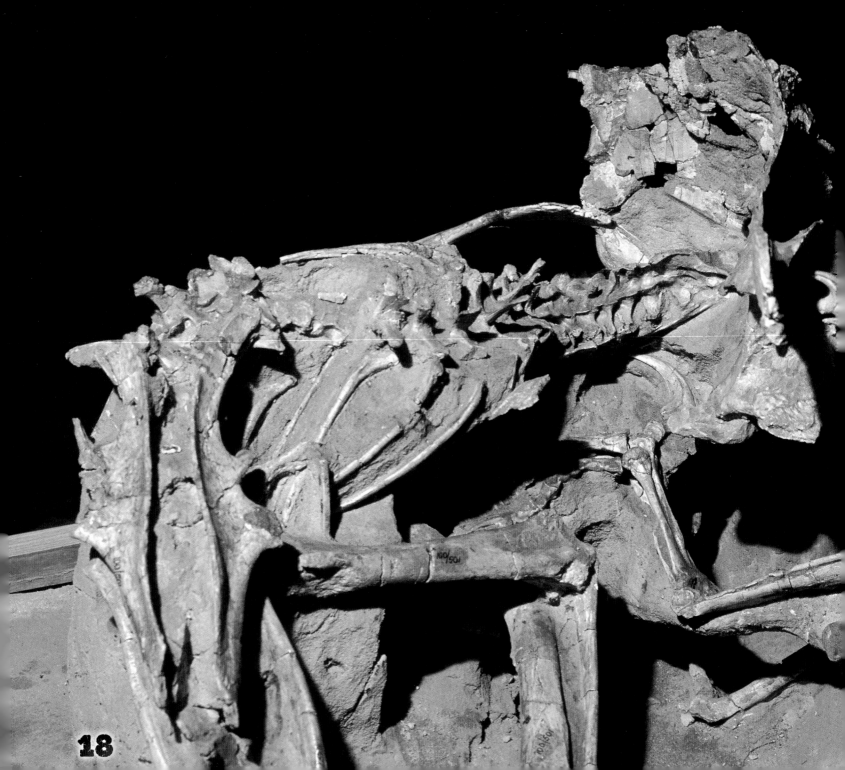

18

Scientists have found *Velociraptor* bones, teeth, and claws. They have also found an awesome *Velociraptor* skeleton. Another dinosaur skeleton was with it. The two were fighting when they died. Their skeletons were still locked in battle! This is one of the best dinosaur discoveries ever.

These fossilized skeletons of Velociraptor *fighting a* Protoceratops *are very famous. The two dinosaurs might have fallen into sand as they were fighting.*

WHERE HAVE VELOCIRAPTOR BONES BEEN FOUND?

Russia

Gobi Desert

Inner Mongolia, China

EUROPE

ASIA

NORTH AMERICA

Atlantic Ocean

Pacific Ocean

AFRICA

SOUTH AMERICA

Indian Ocean

AUSTRALIA

Map Key

Where *Velociraptor* bones have been found

Where possible *Velociraptor* fossils or tracks have been found

Southern Ocean

WHO FINDS THE BONES?

Fossil hunters find dinosaur bones. Some fossil hunters are scientists. Others are people who hunt fossils for fun. They go to areas where dinosaurs once lived. They find bones in rocky places, in mountainsides, and in deserts.

When fossil hunters discover dinosaur bones, they get busy. They use picks to chip rocks away from the fossils. They use small brushes to sweep off any dirt. They take pictures of the fossils. They also write notes about where the fossils were found. They want to remember everything!

Fossil hunters use many tools to dig up fossils. It is very important to use the right tools so the fossils do not get damaged.

GLOSSARY

beast (*BEEST*) A beast is a large wild animal.

discoveries (*diss-KUH-vur-eez*) Discoveries are things that have never been found before.

fossils (FOSS-ullz) Fossils are preserved parts of plants and animals that died long ago.

prey (*PRAY*) An animal that is caught and eaten by another animal is called prey.

Protoceratops (*pro-toe-SAYR-ah-tops*) Protoceratops was a chunky, plant-eating dinosaur.

scientists (*SY-un-tists*) Scientists are people who study how things work through observations and experiments.

skeleton (*SKEL-uh-tun*) The skeleton is the set of bones in a body.

thief (*THEEF*) A thief is a person or animal that steals things.

Velociraptor (*vuh-LAHS-ih-rap-tur*) Velociraptor was a dinosaur that lived about 80 million years ago.

BOOKS

Bentley, Dawn. *Lead the Way, Velociraptor!*
Norwalk, CT: Little Soundprints, 2004.

Bentley, Dawn. *Velociraptor: Small and Speedy.*
Norwalk, CT: Soundprints, 2004.

Landau, Elaine. *Velociraptor*. New York: Children's Press, 2007.

My Terrific Dinosaur Book. New York: DK Publishing, 2008.

Nunn, Daniel. *Velociraptor*. Chicago: Heinemann Library, 2007.

WEB SITES

Visit our Web site for lots of links about *Velociraptor*:
CHILDSWORLD.COM/LINKS

Note to Parents, Teachers, and Librarians: We routinely verify our Web links to make sure they are safe, active sites—so encourage your readers to check them out!

INDEX

ABOUT THE AUTHOR

Susan Gray has written more than ninety books for children. She especially likes to write about animals. Susan lives in Cabot, Arkansas, with her husband, Michael, and many pets.

ABOUT THE ILLUSTRATOR

Robert Squier has been drawing dinosaurs ever since he could hold a crayon. Today, instead of using crayons, he uses pencils, paint, and the computer. Robert lives in New Hampshire with his wife, Jessica, and a house full of dinosaur toys. *Stegosaurus* is his favorite dinosaur.